BOOK OF

Rosemary

BOOK OF
Rosemary

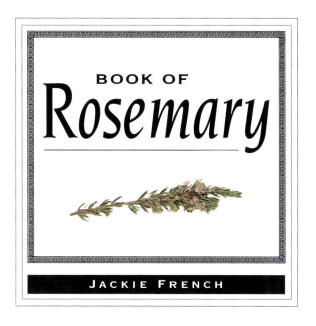

JACKIE FRENCH

HarperCollins*Publishers*

First published in 1993
by HarperCollins Publishers
London

First published in Australia in 1993 by
Angus&Robertson, an imprint of HarperCollins Publishers

© *Jackie French 1993*

A CIP catalogue record for this book is available
from the British Library

ISBN 0 00 412898-2
Printed in Hong Kong

CONTENTS

ROSEMARY

ROSEMARY, THE HERB
YOU CAN'T FORGET

...good for pulses, and for the fallynge sycknesse, and for the cowghe, and good agaynst colde...

~

BOORDE, DIETRY, 1542

Rosemary is aptly named the 'herb of remembrance': it has an unforgettable aroma — whether it's baked with roast lamb or lending its warming properties to a liniment for sore joints. Rosemary's pungency has been exploited for thousands of years in cooking, medicine, and cosmetics.

Rosemary is native to the Mediterranean region, where it can still be found (and smelt) growing wild on banks overlooking the sea. It even grows in desert country — a tough, prickly bush with grey-green foliage that blends in with the often barren country where it grows naturally.

Rosemary was brought to northern Europe by the Romans, who used it in cooking, as a medicine, and in pest control. The English seized on it for all purposes, and it was one of the staples of medieval cooking, suiting the highly flavoured, overspiced dishes of the time. As the art of food preservation improved — and other spices became cheaper as trade improved — rosemary was used more sparingly. Many of the medieval recipes that used rosemary would taste like rheumatism ointment to modern taste buds, so strongly were they scented with rosemary.

There's rosemary, that's for remembrance; pray, love, remember...

~

SHAKESPEARE, *HAMLET*

Marinated Olives

Choose some good black olives and place them in a jar with a little rosemary, a few cloves of garlic and a strip of lemon peel. Fill the remaining space in the jar with olive oil. Leave the olives to marinate for at least a week before eating; or for six months if you can restrain yourself.

Rosemary Bridal Drink

SERVES 4-8

~ 2 cups (16 fl oz) lime juice
~ 2 tbspns rosemary leaves
~ 2 cups sliced strawberries
~ 6 cups (1½ qt) ginger ale
(traditionally ginger wine)
~ sugar and water to taste.

Mix all the ingredients. Don't leave the rosemary leaves in the drink for more than 20 minutes or the taste will be too strong. Scoop them out before serving.

The herb has been linked symbolically with both romance and marriage, and with death, though the theme of remembrance and faithfulness runs through both. Rosemary can bind a pair of lovers; placing a wreath of rosemary at a funeral is a promise that faithfulness would extend beyond the grave.

Rosemary's connections with romance go back a long way. According to English folklore, if a maiden placed a plate of flour under a rosemary bush on midsummer night's eve, her future husband's initials would be written in it. To see your true love in a dream, slip a piece of rosemary under your pillow. Rosemary was used in the Middle Ages as a wedding decoration.

Anne of Cleves wore rosemary as well as gold and rubies in her coronet on her marriage to Henry VIII, and all her wedding chests were said to have been made of rosemary wood. A wedding custom of that time demanded that the wedding guests of the bridal party hold rosemary in their right hands as testimony that the bride was still a virgin. Possibly Anne of Cleves overdid the rosemary as her marriage was annulled, unconsummated.

The bride and groom might dip rosemary in their wine cups to toast each other. Rosemary branches were also gilded for more luxurious occasions. Dried rosemary was laid in the bed linen to ensure faithfulness, and a bride who gave her husband a sprig to hold on their wedding night would ensure that he remained faithful. Another way of ensuring faithfulness was for a bride to place three rosemary leaves in the *Song Of Solomon* passage: 'let him always kiss her with the kisses of his mouth', and place the Bible under her husband's pillow. According to another legend, if a man doesn't like the scent of rosemary, he will be a lousy lover.

Grow it for two ends, it matters not at all
Be't for my bridall or my buriall

~

ROBERT HERRICK

Napoleon is said to have loved rosemary, and he drank rosemary water to sweeten his breath. He ordered that rosemary be thrown on the fires in all his rooms to make them fragrant. Josephine is said to have asked Napoleon to wash in rosemary water before entering her bedchamber.

Napoleon obediently used 162 bottles of rosemary water in the first three months of marriage. Interestingly, an excess of rosemary can lead to convulsions, to which Napoleon was prone — but this may simply be coincidence.

Rosemary is a mild antiseptic; and according to folklore the smoke from burning rosemary will dispel pestilence. In the Middle Ages rosemary was burned to banish the plague (it may have helped by repelling the fleas that leapt from plague-infested rats). Judges burned rosemary in their courtrooms in seventeenth-century England to protect them against jail fever carried by the prisoners brought before them. In fact rosemary tossed on a fire makes a room wonderfully fragrant and dispels the smell of 'dead soot' the next day.

The name rosemary comes from the Latin *rose maris*, the 'dew of the sea', possibly because of rosemary's sea-blue flowers — a hedge of rosemary can be a bank of blue. Rosemary is also said to grow better by the sea. I don't know if this is true, but rosemary (like other aromatic small-leaved plants) does tolerate salt winds far better than other tender-leaved plants.

According to legend rosemary's flowers were once white (and there are still white-flowered cultivars). The flowers turned blue when the Virgin Mary brushed her robe over them on the flight to Egypt. The Virgin Mary is also said to have dried Jesus' clothes on a rosemary bush — which is a lovely place to dry any washing, as the clothes become sweet and scented.

According to French folklore the scent of burning rosemary renews one's energy. Greek students wore garlands of rosemary in their hair. Rosemary is said to grow only in the gardens of the righteous. It is also said that it only grows well in a house where a woman rules.

I lette it runne all over my garden wall, not onlie because my bees love it, but because it's the herb sacred to remembrance, and thereforeto to friendship; whence a sprig of it hath a dumb language.

~

SIR THOMAS MORE, GARDENER AND CHANCELLOR OF ENGLAND

Marinated Cauliflower

SERVES 4–6

Steam a very white cauliflower till almost tender. (You can either leave it whole, which can look spectacular, or cut it into 'flowers'.) Plunge it into cold water.

Marinate the cauliflower in a mixture of ½ cup (4 fl oz) olive oil, 1 tbspn chopped parsley, a little chopped rosemary, 3 tbspns lemon juice, black pepper and 2 chopped dried tomatoes, or chopped, very red capsicum (sweet pepper).

Leave the cauliflower in the marinade for at least 2 hours. Serve cold.

ROSEMARY FOR REMEMBRANCE

Rosemary tea was traditionally drunk to improve a failing memory, and according to recent research at the university of Cincinnati, the scent of rosemary really does stimulate the memory. You may like to keep a sprig on the desk in front of you and rub your fingers in it; or keep a porous unglazed pottery container of rosemary oil in your study; or, as several Japanese companies do, simply waft a little through the air conditioning after lunch to dispel post-prandial drowsiness. Rosemary also has symbolic links with remembrance. In parts of Asia it was apparently grown on ancestors' graves to invoke their guidance. It is traditionally carried on Anzac Day, and wreaths of it are made for Remembrance Day.

CULINARY ROSEMARY

*For other meals they depended largely on bread and butter...most people preferred lard,
especially when it was their own home made lard, flavoured with rosemary leaves.*

~

FLORA THOMPSON, *LARK RISE TO CANDLEFORD*, 1939

Bread with rosemary-flavoured dripping used to be a common
Australian dish — not pig lard, the staple of English villages last
century, but rosemary-scented mutton fat. A roast shoulder or leg of
lamb or mutton was strewn with rosemary, which then flavoured the fat
around it.

Surplus dripping was scooped out from the bottom of the dish, along
with the meaty juices and stray bits of roast pumpkin, and served on
bread. Cholesterol-conscious people may scoff at this now, but it was, in
fact, lower in cholesterol than butter, and as long as it was fresh could
be very good indeed. It's a pity that dishes like dripping-rich French
rilletes are still acceptable, but good old-fashioned bread and dripping
is scorned.

Rosemary Soup

Make a rich stock by boiling chicken bones till the stock is fragrant, then strain the stock well through two thicknesses of cloth. Scatter a very few rosemary leaves into the broth, with a touch of lemon juice. Serve hot.
This is one of the best comforters I know for a head cold.

To make pig lard dripping, the fat was stripped off the pig soon after it was killed and thrown into a copper with a good quantity of water. It was then heated very slowly. The dripping would melt and float on top of the water, where it could be scooped off, and the membranes and other impurities would be left behind. A bunch of rosemary thrown in when it was heating, and strained out later, added to both the flavour and digestibility. Rosemary does aid the digestion but is best taken in culinary doses only, not medicinal ones. Too much rosemary can be toxic.

Rosemary is a strong herb, both in scent and effect, and it is very easy to overdo its use in the kitchen. For most dishes a very few leaves are plenty. In fact the scent of rosemary is often more delicious than the taste, and a branch of rosemary baked near a joint will be enough to flavour it.

Rosemary is a classic herb for roasting. Here are a few suggestions.

~ Place a sprig of rosemary next to roast lamb to take away the woolly taste ('woolly' lamb has been touched by the fleece when it was being skinned, which makes the meat rank).

~ Place a sprig in the oven with a roasting chicken — don't let it touch the chicken or the meat may taste too strongly of rosemary. The aroma in the kitchen will be heavenly.

~ Dip a branch of rosemary in olive oil and use it to baste grilled (broiled) meat or prawns.

~ Throw rosemary into the barbecue fire under grilled (broiled) meat.

Tomatoes with Rosemary and Cream

SERVES 4

Place 2 cups (16 fl oz) of cream in a pan with a very light sprinkle of rosemary leaves. Simmer for 10 minutes. The cream should have thickened. Now add 4 halved tomatoes. Cook till the skins start to wrinkle. Add black pepper to taste. Serve very hot.

GROWING ROSEMARY

There were rose bushes there and lavender and rosemary, and a bush apple tree which bore little red and yellow streaked apples in later summer...

~

FLORA THOMPSON, *LARK RISE TO CANDLEFORD*, 1939.

Rosmarinus officinalis

Rosemary is a hardy perennial, tolerating all but the coldest positions. It tolerates drought, frost (except extreme frost), stony soil, clay — but thrives in good, deep, well-drained soil. If rosemary leaves start to fall, the bush may be getting too much water. Rosemary can't stand wet feet.

Rosemary should not be fed much once it is fully grown — too much feeding can lead to disease. Only young plants need to be fed. A scattering of old hen manure twice a year is enough. As rosemary is a stable plant, that is, it doesn't lose its leaves or continue to grow once it has reached a certain height, its need for nutrients is limited.

Never grow rosemary in the shade as this may cause the leaves to become diseased, or the plant may wilt or get sooty mould which will attract woolly aphids. There's not much you can do to remedy any of these if the bush is in the wrong place. Rosemary is very hardy but once it becomes diseased there is little point in trying to treat it. You will just have to assume that either the bush has been badly injured, perhaps by a lawnmower scraping the stem, or is in the wrong place.

Potatoes with Orange Butter and Rosemary

Toss boiled new potatoes in one part butter, one part orange juice and a little rosemary.

Rosemary Onions

SERVES 4

~ 2 cups (500 grms) small onions, peeled

~ 3 tbspns olive oil

~ 1 tbspn red wine vinegar

~ ½ cup (4 fl oz) water

~ 1 tspn rosemary

~ 1 tspn sugar

Place all the ingredients in a saucepan. Simmer till the water has evaporated and the onions are sweet and shiny. Serve hot or cold.

Rosemary will grow from seed but it is much faster to plant cuttings. Take cuttings from a small, low-down side shoot with a 'heel' of old wood attached, in late summer to late autumn. Push the cutting into sandy soil and keep it moist.

Don't uproot the plant at the first sign of new growth; wait at least six months for good roots to develop, preferably a year. Rosemary can send out new leaves before any root development has taken place.

You can also take tip cuttings of new growth in spring. I have had success just hauling out sticks of rosemary and thrusting them in the ground in autumn or spring. They mostly grow.

Young stems of rosemary can be layered in spring and autumn. These will be ready to lift in six months.

Rosemary is slow growing at first, then it seems to leap away. A good bush will last for thirty years.

WHERE TO GROW ROSEMARY

Rosemary as a Ground Cover

Rosemary can be used to cover an area of sloping ground that is difficult to mow. Either plant it with one of the prostrate or semi-prostrate rosemaries or plant several pieces of rosemary branch in the ground in autumn or spring. In three or four years' time your slope will have become a sea of rosemary. Prostrate rosemary hanging in a curtain down a wall looks wonderful and as the stones heat up the rosemary oil evaporates — the scent seems to float forever.

Rosemary in Paving

Rosemary doesn't form a thick enough sward for a 'herb lawn' but it does smell wonderful when trodden on. Remove every sixth or so paving stone from a terrace or courtyard and plant prostrate rosemary there instead.

Rosemary Pizza

SERVES 2–4

Make a pizza base and place on it a layer of puréed tomato and a layer of mozzarella cheese. Sprinkle on some rosemary, chopped shallots (spring onions, scallions) and sliced black olives. Bake in a very hot oven.

Rosemary and Rhubarb Fool

SERVES 4

~ *3 cups raw rhubarb, chopped*

~ *1 cup (7 oz) sugar*

~ *1 tspn rosemary, chopped*

~ *½ cup (4 fl oz) orange juice*

~ *2 cups whipped cream*

Put all the ingredients into a pan and let them simmer until the rhubarb is soft. Blend the stewed rhubarb briefly with the whipped cream, so it swirls together, rather than amalgamates. Serve at once.

Rosemary in the Driveway

This is another good place for prostrate rosemary. You don't have to mow it, rarely have to water it, and it can be neatly trimmed.

Rosemary around the Clothes Line

Plant four rosemary bushes around the base of the clothes line. When they are tall enough to form a hedge keep them neatly trimmed flat, and dry your handkerchiefs or other small items on them.

Rosemary in Pots

Rosemary grows well in pots, as long as they are in a sunny place and
not overwatered. (Don't place them next to moisture- and humidity-
loving maidenhair ferns.) They won't grow as large as bushes outside, of
course, but you will have the scent of rosemary even if you don't have a
garden. Rosemary does best if it is repotted every two to three years.
Prostrate rosemary looks lovely trailing from a tall pot. I have also seen
old drain-pipes filled with soil, then planted with prostrate rosemary.
After about six years the pipes were almost covered with a 'cloth' of
grey-green fragrance.

A Rosemary Hedge

Rosemary is a prickly plant — a thick hedge of it will keep out most animals and is a wonderful shelter for small nesting birds. Bees also love rosemary hedges and when they are flowering the buzz from a rosemary hedge can be heard from afar.

To grow a rosemary hedge, plant dwarf or bush rosemary plants or cuttings about 2 m (78 in) apart and trim them once the branches start to touch. The more you trim the top the thicker the growth will be.

For the more casual gardener, rosemary hedges need not even be trimmed — though they are certainly neater if they are. Keep the prunings and throw them on the fire, or use them as bedding for the dog, to help repel fleas and flies. Don't compost them; rosemary's high oil content will inhibit the break-down of the compost.

For a really neat hedge, grow rosemary bushes with a tightly strained wire in the middle. This will keep the bushes upright.

A Sweet-smelling Perfume

Take a pound of fresh-gathered Orange flowers, of common Roses, Lavender seeds and Musk Roses, each half a pound; of Sweet Marjoram Leaves and Clove-July flowers picked, each quarter of a pound; of Thyme, three ounces; of Myrtle leaves and Melilot Stalks stripped of their leaves, each two ounces; of Rosemary Leaves, and Cloves bruised, each an ounce; of Bay Leaves, half an ounce.

Let these ingredients be mixed in a large pan covered with parchment and be exposed to the heat of the sun during the whole summer for the first month, stirring them every other day with a stick, and taking them within doors in rainy weather. Towards the end of the season they will afford an excellent composition for perfume; which may be rendered yet more fragrant, by adding a little scented Cypress-powder, mixed with coarse Violet Powder.

~

The Toilet of Flora, *1775*

PRESERVING ROSEMARY

Rosemary is really too pungent to be used in herbal oils or vinegars and
after prolonged seeping the oil smells like liniment. It is best dried.
Dried rosemary loses almost none of the power or subtle undertones of
fresh rosemary.
Rosemary is at its most pungent when it is flowering. Harvest rosemary
for drying soon after the dew has dried (and make sure the plant really
is dry, or the leaves may rot). Then hang the herb in small bunches in
an airy spot, out of strong light. Make sure the place is warm and airy
— if rosemary dries too slowly much of the fragrance will be lost.
You can crumble the dried herb into pots, or hang long branches over
the stove, to help fragrance the kitchen.

Rosemary Jelly

This is good served with cold roast lamb.

~ 2 kg (4 lb) apples, cut into quarters
~ 2 cups (16 fl oz) water
~ 2 tbspns rosemary
~ sugar
~ lemon juice

Simmer the apples in the water until they start to break up and form a sludge. Add the rosemary while the apples are still hot. Strain the apples through a teatowel or muslin, twice. The resulting apple purée will be clear, and rosemary scented.

For every cup (8 oz) of purée, add 1 cup (7 oz) of white sugar and the juice of half a lemon. Simmer until the sugar is dissolved and a little jelly tested in cold water sets into a blob (this will take about 5 minutes).

Fill into small clean jars and seal well.

The following rosemaries are all commercially available. While many other forms, including silver and gold coloured rosemaries, are referred to in old texts, they are very rare today.

Bush Rosemary
(Rosmarinus officinalis)

The standard rosemary bush. It will grow to 1–1.5 m (3–4 ft) high, with pale blue flowers in late spring and early summer, though there are also white-and pink-flowered cultivars available.

Bush rosemary is the best hedging rosemary, fast growing and hardy. Dwarf bush rosemary is a smaller version of bush rosemary, suitable for edging the garden. It has slightly brighter blue flowers than the taller rosemary.

Spaghetti Sauce

SERVES 2–4

~ ½ cup (4 fl oz) olive oil

~ 1 cup dried tomatoes, chopped

~ ⅓ cup (2 oz) black olives

~ 6 garlic cloves, chopped

~ 1 tspn rosemary

~ chopped parsley

Place all the ingredients in a pan and allow to simmer for a few minutes. Mix into very good spaghetti.

This isn't the usual thick and meaty spaghetti sauce — it is oily, but good. The quality depends on having good spaghetti, good oil and good dried tomatoes.

Prostrate Rosemary
(Rosmarinus officinalis *var.* prostratus)

This has similar scent and growing habits to bush rosemary, but instead of growing upwards it creeps along the ground. It is extremely flat-looking for a variant of such a prickly, upright plant — and it gives the effect of seeping, like a blue green wave, in and out of stones in rockeries and across paving stones. The flowers are deep, bright blue in summer.

Rosmarinus officinalis
'Lockward de Forest'

Another prostrate form, also with bright blue flowers.

Fillet of Lamb with Rosemary Sauce

SERVES 4

Brown the fillet in olive oil, then roast in a moderate oven for about 20 minutes. The meat should be brown outside and pink inside. Serve it thinly sliced with rosemary sauce:

ROSEMARY SAUCE:

Mix 4 cups (1 qt) good meat stock with 1 cup (8 fl oz) Madeira and a few rosemary leaves. Simmer for about 1 hour until thickened, then pour the mixture into the pan with the meat juices and boil well for another three minutes. Note: Stock cubes won't give the right result — a good meat stock will thicken and turn shiny as it reduces.

Rosmarinus officinalis
'Benenden Blue'

A semi-prostrate form of bush rosemary with vivid deep blue flowers that may appear in autumn or spring, or even in winter in mild areas. 'Benenden Blue' rosemary is an excellent garden edging plant, and wonderful to let sprawl down banks and walls. 'Blue Lagoon' may be another name for 'Benenden Blue', although they are often listed separately. 'Blue Lagoon' is sold in both a bush and prostrate form and is fast growing with bright blue flowers.

Rosmarinus officinalis
'Grey Lady'

The flowers of this rosemary are grey-white, faintly striped with lavender. The leaves are strongly fragrant and delicate.

Rosmarinus officinalis 'Blue Lagoon'

Marinated Lamb Kebabs

SERVES 4

Cut the meat from a leg of lamb into small chunks. Marinate in a mixture of 2 cups (16 fl oz) natural yoghurt, 4 chopped cloves of garlic, the juice of 2 lemons and a few leaves of rosemary. Thread the meat onto skewers and grill (broil) it.

Rosemary Hearth Cakes

~ 2 cups (8 oz) self-raising (self-rising) flour

~ 125 g (4 oz) butter

~ ½ cup (3 oz) soft brown sugar

~ ½ cup (2½ oz) currants

~ 1 egg

~ 1 tbspn chopped rosemary

Mix all the ingredients into a dough. Roll out the dough and then cut into thin rounds. Fry over low heat until pale gold and puffy. There is no need to grease the pan — there is enough butter in the hearthcakes.

Rosmarinus officinalis
'Tradescant'

This is said to be a sixteenth-century rosemary, with pale blue flowers
flecked with dark blue. The leaves are deep green.

ROSEMARY AND COMPANION PLANTING

Like many plants high in oil, rosemary can suppress the growth of plants that grow under it, where they may be affected by the oil from the leaves. Prostrate rosemary, on the other hand, forms a lovely carpet under roses.

If you live by the sea and your plants are stunted by the salt winds, grow a rosemary hedge around the garden to shelter it and help catch the salt.

*Chicken with Rosemary
and Tomato*

SERVES 4

~ 8 chicken pieces

~ 1 slice bacon, chopped

~ 2 tbspns olive oil

~ 1 cup (8 fl oz) red wine

~ 8 tomatoes, peeled and
chopped (or 2 x 410 g/14 oz
cans of tomatoes)

~ 1 tspn rosemary

~ 6 garlic cloves

*Sauté the chicken and bacon in
olive oil until the chicken is
brown. Add the red wine;
simmer for 3 minutes. Place
in a casserole and add the
tomatoes, rosemary and garlic.
Put the lid on the casserole
and cook slowly until the
chicken is tender and the
sauce thick.*

ROSEMARY AND ANIMALS

Rosemary is said to enhance the flavour of the
meat of an animal that has grazed on it, and to
improve the flavour of milk as well. In the
Middle East powdered rosemary is said to be
sprinkled on the umbilical cord of newborn
animals to help prevent infection, and Arab and
Spanish horse masters were said to use powdered
rosemary as a wound dressing.

A strong rosemary tea is used as an insecticide,
and rosemary oil is rubbed into inflamed joints to
relieve the pain of arthritis or rheumatism.

Bags of rosemary and bran can be heated to
soothe bruises and swellings, and help 'draw out'
infection.

ROSEMARY AS A PEST REPELLENT

Rosemary oil will help repel mosquitoes, if you don't mind smelling of roast lamb. Dried branches of rosemary in your cupboards will help keep away moths and silverfish, though lavender is more effective.

Quail with Rosemary and Orange Sauce

SERVES 4

~ 8 quail (or substitute chicken pieces or duck quarters)

~ 4 tbspns olive oil

~ 4 garlic cloves, chopped

~ 1 tspn ground cardamon

~ 1 cup (8 fl oz) white wine

~ 3 bay leaves

~ 1 tspn honey

~ 1 tbspn grated orange rind

~ juice of 3 oranges

~ 2 tbspns chopped shallots (spring onions, scallions)

~ 1 tspn rosemary.

Brown the quail in the heated olive oil. Add the garlic and cardamon. When the cardamon is browned, add the white wine and simmer for 3 minutes. Add the remaining ingredients, place in a baking dish and bake in a moderate oven (190°C/375°F) for about 30 minutes, or until the birds are cooked.

Remove the birds, and allow the sauce to bubble until it thickens. Serve the sauce either poured over the birds, or in a sauceboat.

MEDICINAL ROSEMARY

Rosemary is a plant of great service in Affections of the Head and Nerves, helping the apoplexy, Palsy and all kinds of convulsions...it strengthens the sight and the memory...

~

JOSEPH MILLER, *GARDENER'S DICTIONARY*, 1732

Rosemary oil is added to liniments for muscular aches and rheumatism, as well as for the cosmetic preparations listed elsewhere. It is also slightly antiseptic and is added to baths and used in a diluted form to cleanse grazes. It is rarely used internally as large doses can be toxic, and it can also lead to miscarriage. One safe preparation (though pregnant women should still avoid it) is rosemary honey, which acts as an expectorant.

Rosemary, sage and coltsfoot were the main ingredients in a herbal tobacco for asthmatics. I don't recommend it.

Rosemary oil is said to relieve a headache if rubbed on the temples.

Rosemary Honey

Heat 1 cup (8 fl oz) honey with 1 cup rosemary leaves for 5 minutes. Strain and place in a jar. Leave for 2 weeks then heat and strain again. Take 1 teaspoonful 3 times a day.

Baked Apples with Rosemary

Place 4 Granny Smith apples or other cooking apples in a pan (with the skin of the apples scored lightly to prevent them bursting). Cover with a glass of red wine, a few rosemary leaves and lots of brown sugar. Bake till soft. Serve with masses of whipped cream.

ROSEMARY COSMETICS

Take the flowers of rosemary and put them in Lynen clothe, and so boyle them in fayre cleane
water to the halfe and cole it and drynke it for it is much worth against all the evyls in the body.

~

ANONYMOUS, *A LYTEL HERBALL*, 1550

Rosemary has a long history of cosmetic use, from the Egyptians to the
gypsies, who used it for skin and hair. Rosemary oil is said to prevent
crow's-feet if rubbed around the eyes; it improves skin tone, is used in
perfumery, and is a wonderful conditioner for the hair.

The distilled water of the floures of rosemary being drunke at morning and evening first and
late, taketh away the stench of the mouth and breath, and make it very sweet...

~

JOHN GERARD, *HERBAL*, (1545–1612)

ROSEMARY IN PERFUMERY

Hungary Water

According to her own story, Donna Izabella,
Queen of Hungary, was severely afflicted with
gout. At the age of 72 she was visited by a
wandering hermit, who left her the recipe for
Hungary Water. In the words of the Queen, 'I
recovered my health and regained my strength,
and on beholding my beauty the king of Poland
desired to marry me; which I refused for the love
of our Lord Jesus Christ, believing that the
receipt had been given me by an angel.'

*A Recipe for Hungary
Water*

*Place in a jar 1 tbspn mint
leaves, 1 tbspn rosemary
leaves, ½ cup fragrant rose
petals and the grated rind
(without pith) of 1 orange
and 1 lemon. Fill the jar with
brandy and seal the jar. Leave
for at least a week, shaking
every day. Store in dark,
well-sealed bottles.*

Eau de Cologne

*Place in a large jar the grated
rind (no pith) of 1 orange
2 tbspns bergamot leaves, the
grated peel of 2 lemons (no
pith) and 4 tbspns rosemary
leaves. Fill the jar with
brandy and seal the jar.
Shake every day for 3 weeks.
Strain out the cologne.*

ROSEMARY AND HAIR CARE

Rosemary oil can be added straight to the hair (it won't make it greasy). It gives gloss and richness.

Dry Shampoo

Take 1 part orris root, 1 part ground dried rosemary and 1 part arrowroot flour. Dry them thoroughly in a slow oven, grind to a powder and brush through the hair. Leave for 10 minutes then brush out again. The powder should take both grease and dirt with it.

Rosemary Shampoo

Simmer 2 cups rosemary in 3 cups (24 fl oz) water for 10 minutes. Strain and add ⅓ cup saponified coconut oil (found in health food shops) and 3 tspns of glycerin. Shake well.
This recipe gives me dandruff, but other people love it.

Another Rosemary Shampoo

Simmer for 10 minutes 6 cups of soapwort (leaves, stems and roots), ½ cup rosemary and 3 cups (24 fl oz) water. Cool and strain.

Hair Conditioner for Dry Hair

Half fill a glass jar with rosemary leaves. Top it up with sunflower oil. Let it steep in the sunlight for at least a week, shaking regularly. Rub the oil through the hair 10 minutes before washing.

Another Rosemary Hair Conditioner

Put a few drops of rosemary oil on your hairbrush and brush your hair well to distribute the oil evenly.

Rosemary Setting Lotion

Boil 2 tbspns of flax seed, or 2 tbspns of quince seeds with 2 tbspns of rosemary in 2 cups (16 fl oz) of water for 30 minutes (you may need to add more water). This is best for dark hair.

To Wash Hairbrushes

Simmer 1 cup rosemary leaves with 3 cups (24 fl oz) water and ½ cup (4 fl oz) cider vinegar for 20 minutes. Strain out the leaf remnants and use the liquid to wash your brushes to free them of grease and leave them sweet smelling. (This may also help repel — but not kill — head lice.)

Rosemary Oil and Head Lice

Rosemary oil is sometimes sold or recommended to kill head lice (head lice eggs are called 'nits'). Rosemary oil doesn't kill head lice, though any oil rubbed through the hair may make it a little easier to remove the nits by hand, using tweezers and a fine comb.

BATHING WITH ROSEMARY

A little rosemary oil added to the bathwater is said to be invigorating and to help ease aches and soothe scratches. Don't use it in the bath before going to bed — it may keep you awake.

Herbal Bath Bag

Combine in a small cotton or towelling bag 2 cups (6 oz) rolled oats, ½ cup
(2 oz) ground almonds and ½ cup rosemary leaves.
Use the bag as a combination of soap and sponge. It will last for at least
a week's bathing.

Rosemary Foot-Bath

Simmer for 10 minutes 2 cups (16 fl oz) cider vinegar, ½ cup rosemary flowers
and 3 tbspns camomile flowers.
This is especially good for tired or smelly feet.

Bath Oils

Bath oils rarely contain more than a few drops of oil, which are added
merely for perfume. Few oils disperse in water and a pure 'oil' additive
would leave a greasy mess on both the bath and its occupant.
To make a simple 'bath oil', use any fragrant flowers — dianthus are
excellent — or musk roses, carnations, jasmine, pittosporum or boronia
flowers, or any fragrant leaves, such as scented geranium, mints or
verbena. Chop them roughly, place in a jar and add a sliver of soap. Fill
with water, put on the lid and leave in a hot place like the bathroom
windowsill till required. Shake the bottle every time you pass by.
To use simply empty the scented soapy water into the bath.

After Shower Cologne

Take 1 cup rosemary leaves, add some chopped lemon or lime or orange
peel and a little mint. Chop roughly, squash it down in a jar, barely
cover with brandy, put on the lid and leave overnight. Next morning
top up with boiling water and reseal.
Leave for a week. Strain out the liquid, put it into an airtight jar or
bottle and seal the jar. Shake well before use.

HOME-MADE PERSONAL DEODORANTS

There are many home-made deodorants, but none will stop perspiration — perspiration helps cool and cleanse the body — and none will be as effective as a deodorant containing aluminium.

Rosemary Deodorant

Combine equal parts cider vinegar and rosemary oil. Dab on.

Herbal Vinegar Deodorant

Stuff a jar with rosemary leaves, lavender flowers and thyme leaves. Fill the jar with hot cider vinegar. Put the lid on. Steep overnight. Dab the vinegar on when needed.

Rosemary and Lemon Deodorant

Stuff a jar with rosemary leaves interlayered with slices of lemon. Fill the jar with water.
Leave for 3 weeks. Now scrunch the whole mixture up in your hands. You'll be left with a pulpy mess. Strain it, and bottle the liquid. Keep it in the refrigerator. Dab on as needed. Don't put your clothes on until the deodorant dries.

MAKING THE HOUSE FRAGRANT

Evaporating Oils

Place a dish of water with a few drops of rosemary oil over a light bulb — or add a few drops of oil to a saucepan of simmering water (use the lowest possible heat).

Toilet Odours

Place a bowl of rosemary potpourri above the toilet.
Combine 6 cups dried rosemary, 1 cup dried mint, the dried rind of 2 oranges and 2 lemons, a little cinnamon and ½ cup orris root.

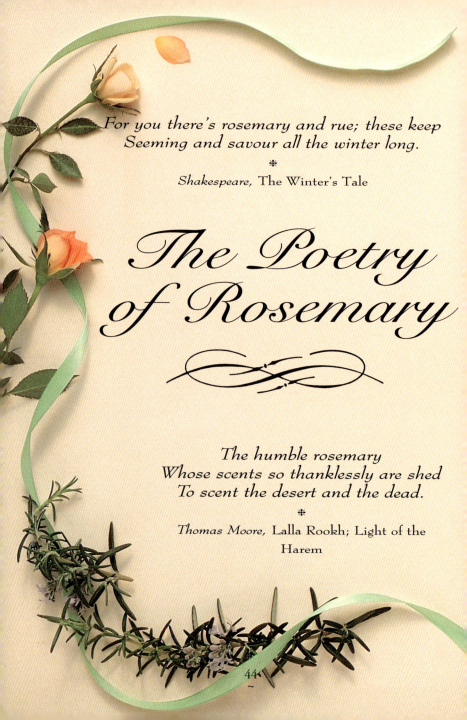

For you there's rosemary and rue; these keep
Seeming and savour all the winter long.

*

Shakespeare, The Winter's Tale

The Poetry
of Rosemary

The humble rosemary
Whose scents so thanklessly are shed
To scent the desert and the dead.

*

Thomas Moore, Lalla Rookh; Light of the
Harem

Take what quantity you will of the flowers and put them into a strong glass close stopped, tie a fine linen cloth over the mouth, and turn the mouth down into another strong glass, which being set in the sun, an oil will distill down into the lower glass, to be preserved as precious for divers uses, both inward and outward, as a soverign balm to heal the diseases before mentioned, to clean dim sight, and take away spots, marks, and scars in the skin.

*

Culpeper

Rosemary is for remembrance
Between us day and night
Wishing that I might always have
You present in my sight

*

Thomas Robinson Nosegay for Lovers *(1584)*

AND FINALLY...
AN ANCIENT ROMAN ROSEMARY
APHRODISIAC

Take dried rose and violet petals, saffron, myrrh, lavender and rosemary.
Mix with an equal quantity of dried viper's flesh (red-bellied black
snake, or your own local poisonous snake, may do, but avoid the poison
glands near the head!) and steep in honey.

ACKNOWLEDGMENTS

The publisher would like to thank the following organisations in New South Wales, Australia, for supplying various photographic props:

The Fragrant Garden, Erina

Grosvenor Antique Centre, Lindfield

Sweet Violets, Lindfield

Home & Garden on the Mall, Sky Gardens, Sydney

Wild Australia, Sky Gardens, Sydney

Linen & Lace, Balmain

~ ~ ~

PHOTOGRAPHY
Scott Cameron Photography Pty Ltd

FOOD STYLING
Lisa Hilton

COVER PHOTOGRAPHY
Ivy Hansen